EAGLES

Published by Creative Education, Inc., 123 South Broad Street, Mankato, Minnesota
56001

Printed by permission of Wildlife Education, Ltd.

ISBN 0-88682-225-4

EAGLES

Created and Written by
John Bonnett Wexo

Zoological Consultant
Charles R. Schroeder, D.V.M.
Director Emeritus
San Diego Zoo &
San Diego Wild Animal Park

Scientific Consultants
David H. Ellis, Ph. D.
Research Director
Institute for Raptor Studies

Amadeo M. Rea, Ph. D.
Curator of Birds and Mammals
San Diego Natural History Museum

Creative Education

Art Credits

Pages Eight and Nine: Trevor Boyer; **Pages Ten and Eleven:** Trevor Boyer; **Page Ten: Top Right, Middle Left, and Bottom Right,** Walter Stuart; **Page Eleven: Middle Left and Bottom,** Walter Stuart; **Pages Twelve and Thirteen:** Trevor Boyer; **Page Twelve: Middle Right, Middle Left, and Bottom Right,** Walter Stuart; **Page Thirteen: Middle Right and Left,** Walter Stuart; **Bottom Left and Center,** Walter Stuart; **Pages Sixteen and Seventeen:** Trevor Boyer; **Page Seventeen: Bottom Right,** Walter Stuart; **Pages Eighteen and Nineteen:** Trevor Boyer; **Pages Twenty and Twenty-One:** Trevor Boyer; **Page Twenty: Bottom Left,** Walter Stuart; **Page Twenty-One: Middle Right,** Walter Stuart.

Photographic Credits

Cover: J.J.G. Grande *(Bruce Coleman, Ltd.)*; **Pages Six and Seven:** Gunter Ziesler *(Bruce Coleman, Ltd.)*; **Page Thirteen:** Med Beauregard *(PPS)*; **Pages Fourteen and Fifteen:** Gunter Ziesler *(Bruce Coleman, Ltd.)*; **Page Seventeen: Top Left,** Joe VanWormer *(Photo Researchers)*; **Middle Right,** Charlie Ott *(Photo Researchers)*; **Bottom Center,** Dr. Harold Edgerton *(MIT, Cambridge, MA)*; **Page Eighteen: Bottom Left,** R. & M. Borland *(Bruce Coleman, Ltd.)*; **Bottom Right,** Norman Myers *(Bruce Coleman, Inc.)*; **Page Nineteen: Top Left,** Jeff Foott *(Survival Anglia)*; **Middle Right,** Souricat *(Animals Animals)*; **Page Twenty: Top Right,** Kent R. Keller; **Middle Left,** Johnny Johnson *(DRK Photo)*; **Page Twenty-One: Top Left,** Kent R. Keller; **Bottom Left,** David Ellis; **Pages Twenty-Two and Twenty-Three:** Jim Reardon *(Alaska Photo)*.

Our Thanks To: Ray Barnes; Martine Culbertson *(VIREO)*; Dr. Jerry Johns; Peter Johnson; Dr. & Mrs. Bruce Lang; Charmion R. McKusick; Jean Mooney *(MIT)*; Kerry Muller *(San Diego Zoo)*; Debra Prather; Elizabeth Weidenkeller; Dr. Richard Zusi *(Smithsonian Institution)*.

This book is dedicated to Lynnette Medina Wexo, whose intellect, creativity, and unflagging patience have been essential to the creation of Wildlife Education, Ltd. and of every Zoobook.

Creative Education would like to thank Wildlife Education, Ltd., for granting them the rights to print and distribute this hardbound edition.

Contents

Eagles have always been admired by people. This is partly because some eagles are big and powerful. It is partly because many eagles are very beautiful. And it is partly because *all* eagles are wonderful flyers. Many people have found themselves looking up in wonder at an eagle circling high in the sky.

When most people think of eagles, they think of big birds. So it is a surprise to discover that there are eagles of many different sizes, from very small to very large. The smallest eagle is probably the Little eagle of Australia. When these birds spread their wings, the wingspan—the distance from wingtip to wingtip—is only about 3 feet (92 centimeters). And they weigh only a little more than one pound (483 grams).

The biggest of the eagles is very much bigger. Female Harpy eagles from South America can be truly huge. They may weigh over 20 pounds (9 kilograms), and their legs may be as big around as a child's wrist. (As with most eagles, the female is larger than the male, and the male Harpy weighs only about 10 pounds.)

Whatever their sizes may be, all eagles are top predators. This means that they eat other animals, but other animals seldom eat them. Eagles catch fish, mammals, and other birds—and they are all very good hunters. You could say that these powerful birds are like lions with wings.

The fact that eagles kill other animals upsets some people. But it's good to remember that eagles aren't doing it to be cruel. Like lions, they are only doing what they are supposed to be doing. It is their *job* in nature to eat other animals.

Eagles and other predators help to keep the natural world in balance. If there were no predators, the numbers of other animals would quickly get out of hand. There would soon be too many animals for the amount of food available. And then many animals would die of starvation. The predators take *some* animals so that *many* can stay alive and healthy.

There are eagles on every continent in the world except Antarctica. And they live in many different kinds of habitats. You can find eagles in deserts, jungles, swamps, and forests. Some live down by the ocean and some live up in the mountains.

All eagles are diurnal (DIE-URN-ul). This means that they hunt during the day and sleep at night. Some of the larger eagles have lived longer than 40 years in zoos, but in the wild they probably live only about 20 years.

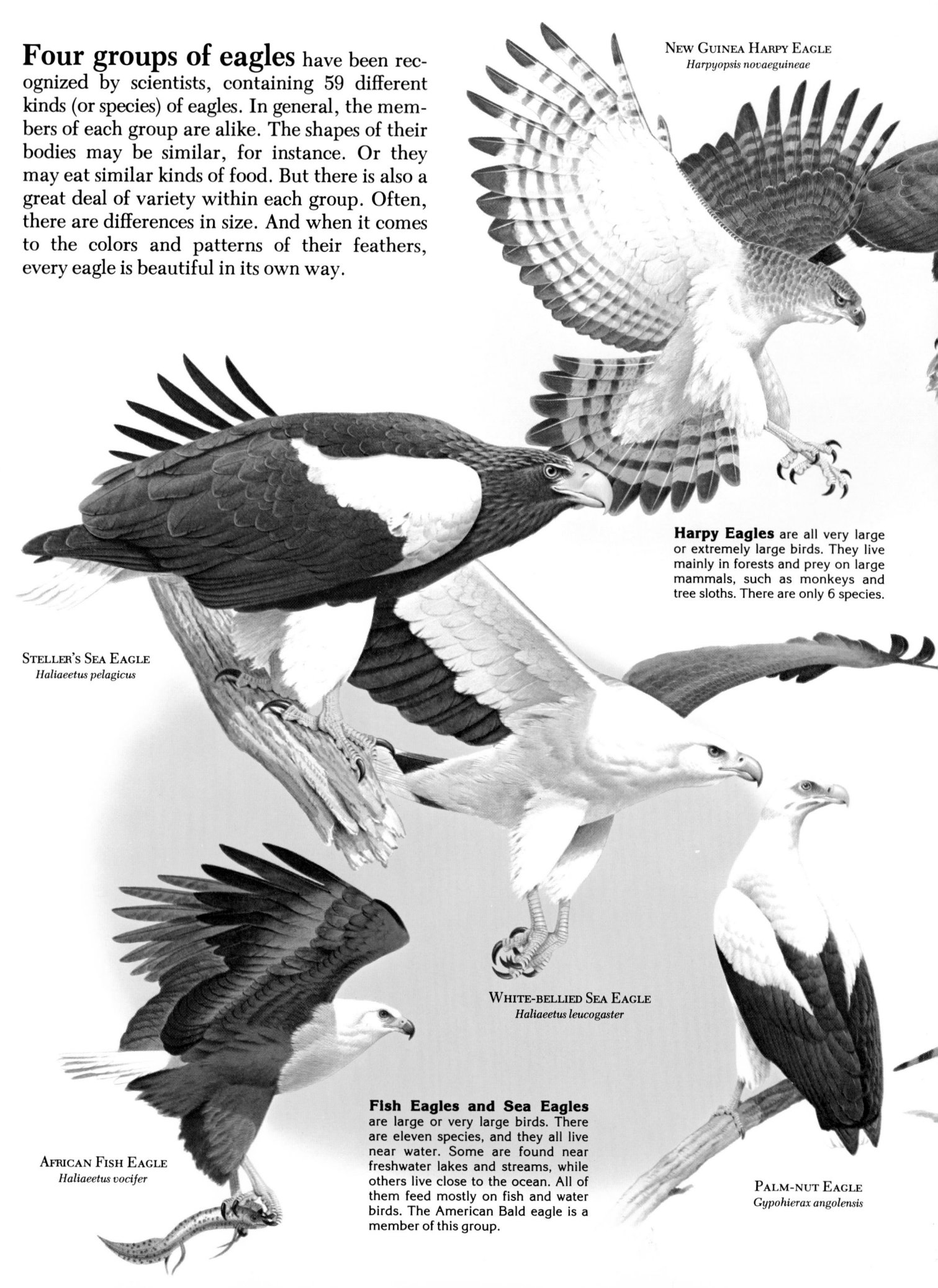

Four groups of eagles have been recognized by scientists, containing 59 different kinds (or species) of eagles. In general, the members of each group are alike. The shapes of their bodies may be similar, for instance. Or they may eat similar kinds of food. But there is also a great deal of variety within each group. Often, there are differences in size. And when it comes to the colors and patterns of their feathers, every eagle is beautiful in its own way.

NEW GUINEA HARPY EAGLE
Harpyopsis novaeguineae

Harpy Eagles are all very large or extremely large birds. They live mainly in forests and prey on large mammals, such as monkeys and tree sloths. There are only 6 species.

STELLER'S SEA EAGLE
Haliaeetus pelagicus

WHITE-BELLIED SEA EAGLE
Haliaeetus leucogaster

AFRICAN FISH EAGLE
Haliaeetus vocifer

Fish Eagles and Sea Eagles are large or very large birds. There are eleven species, and they all live near water. Some are found near freshwater lakes and streams, while others live close to the ocean. All of them feed mostly on fish and water birds. The American Bald eagle is a member of this group.

PALM-NUT EAGLE
Gypohierax angolensis

CROWNED SOLITARY EAGLE
Harpyhaliaetus coronatus

BATELEUR
Terathopius ecaudatus

CRESTED SERPENT EAGLE
Spilornis cheela

Snake Eagles are small to medium-sized birds. They hunt snakes most of the time, but will eat lizards and frogs. There are 12 species, and they are found in areas where snakes live—in forests and deserts, and on the plains.

CELEBES SERPENT EAGLE
Spilornis rufipectus

LONG-CRESTED EAGLE
Spizaetus occipitalis

BONELLI'S EAGLE
Hieraeetus fasciatus

BLACK & WHITE HAWK EAGLE
Spizastur melanoleucos

GOLDEN EAGLE
Aquila chrysaetos

VERREAUX'S EAGLE
Aquila verreauxi

Booted Eagles come in many different sizes, from small to large. Unlike other eagles, all the members of this group have feathers on their legs that extend down to the feet like "boots." There are 30 species, and there are members of this group living almost everywhere in the world that eagles *can* live. They live in the Arctic and in tropical forests, in low areas and the highest mountains.

ORNATE HAWK EAGLE
Spizaetus ornatus

9

The body of an eagle is made for flying and for catching prey. To do these things, the body must be light in weight and very strong. It must be light enough to get off the ground and fly high in the air, but strong enough to swoop down on prey and carry it away.

It is really amazing to see the many ways in which an eagle's body combines low weight with high strength. There doesn't seem to be an extra ounce of weight anywhere. For example, the feathers on a large eagle can be very sturdy—but each feather weighs *next to nothing*. A Bald eagle has more than 7 thousand feathers, but all of them put together weigh less than 21 ounces (586 grams). If you took 30 of these feathers in your hand, they would weigh *less than a penny*.

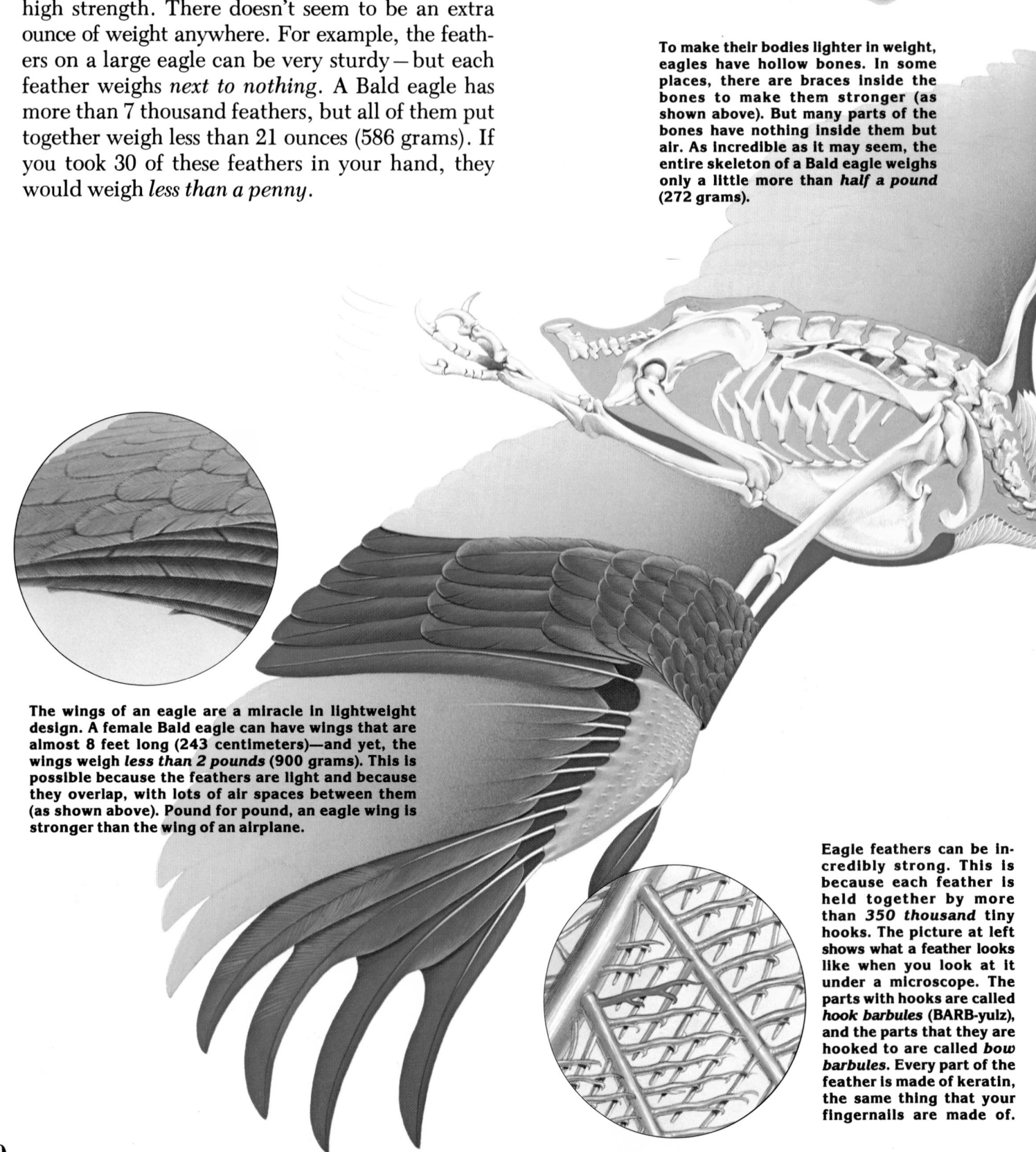

Human Bone

Eagle Bone

To make their bodies lighter in weight, eagles have hollow bones. In some places, there are braces inside the bones to make them stronger (as shown above). But many parts of the bones have nothing inside them but air. As incredible as it may seem, the entire skeleton of a Bald eagle weighs only a little more than *half a pound* (272 grams).

The wings of an eagle are a miracle in lightweight design. A female Bald eagle can have wings that are almost 8 feet long (243 centimeters)—and yet, the wings weigh *less than 2 pounds* (900 grams). This is possible because the feathers are light and because they overlap, with lots of air spaces between them (as shown above). Pound for pound, an eagle wing is stronger than the wing of an airplane.

Eagle feathers can be incredibly strong. This is because each feather is held together by more than *350 thousand* tiny hooks. The picture at left shows what a feather looks like when you look at it under a microscope. The parts with hooks are called *hook barbules* (BARB-yulz), and the parts that they are hooked to are called *bow barbules*. Every part of the feather is made of keratin, the same thing that your fingernails are made of.

When an eagle flaps its wings, most of the power for flying comes from the downward stroke of the wings. For this reason, the muscles that pull the wings down ① are much larger than the muscles that pull the wings up ②. The flight muscles are so important to an eagle that they often account for half of the bird's total weight.

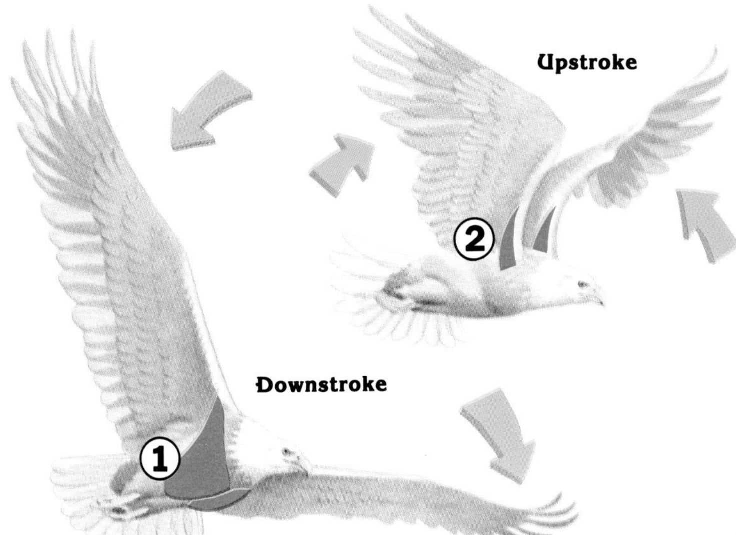

Upstroke

Downstroke

② ①

SEE FOR YOURSELF:

Ⓐ   Ⓑ

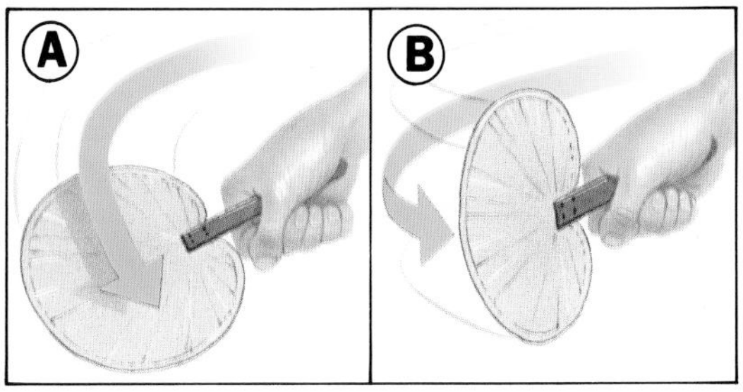

An eagle can fly faster or slower by changing the position of its wings. When it wants to fly fast, it turns the front edges of the wings into the wind and "cuts through" the air, like the fan at left Ⓐ. When the eagle wants to slow itself down, it turns the wide surface of the wings into the wind. The wings "drag" through the air, like the fan at right Ⓑ. Get a fan or a piece of cardboard and try it out.

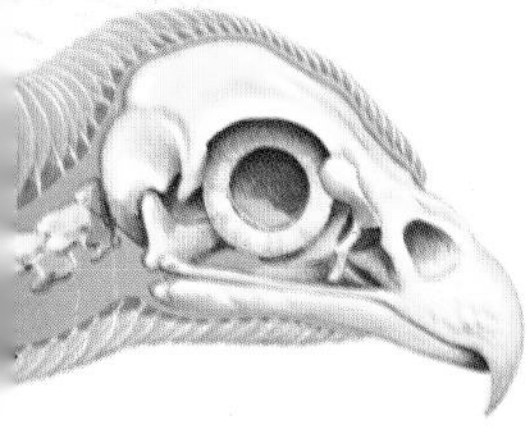

There is no room for a sloppy landing on top of a tall tree or on a cliff, so eagles have to be good at landing. To slow themselves for a landing, they spread their wings and tail down, and "drag" them through the air (like fan Ⓑ at left).

SEE FOR YOURSELF:

It's easy to understand how an eagle flies. In general, it is the air flowing over the top of the wing that lifts the bird into the air. To see how this works, get a piece of paper and hold it as shown below. When you blow gently on the top of the paper, the loose end of the paper will start to move up in the air. Blow harder and the paper will rise higher—and this is exactly what happens with an eagle's wing. The faster that air moves over the top of the wing, the more the wing wants to rise—or, as scientists say, the more "lift" the wing has. When the amount of lift is greater than the weight of the eagle, the bird floats up into the air.

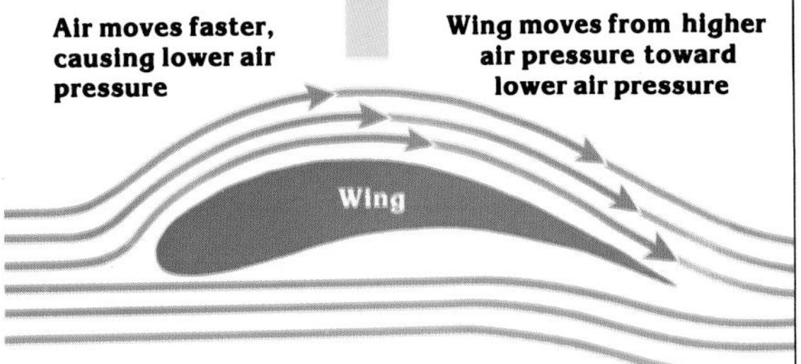

Air moves faster, causing lower air pressure

Wing moves from higher air pressure toward lower air pressure

Wing

Higher Air Pressure

Next, hold the paper up in front of your face and blow on it. The force of your breath hitting the paper is called *air pressure*. As you blow, the paper moves away from you, because the air pressure is greater on your side of the paper than it is on the other side. The paper moves from higher air pressure toward lower air pressure— *and so does a wing*. The fast-moving air on top of the wing lowers the air pressure there, and the wing moves toward the lower pressure—it moves *up*.

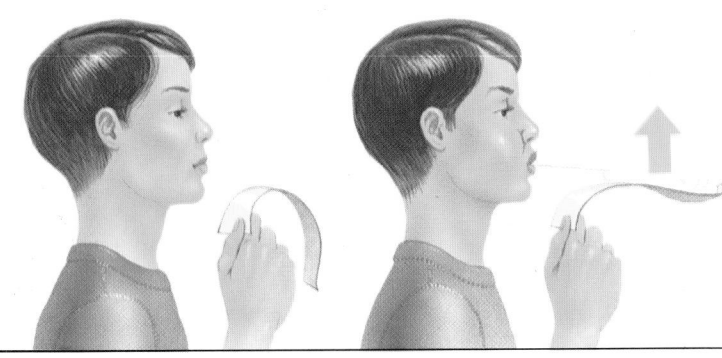

The wings of eagles are powerful, and eagles often use them with great skill. Eagles know how to climb high into the air without working too hard. They know how to float thousands of feet above the ground, without flapping their wings at all. They can swoop down on prey at incredible speeds. And once they have caught it, they can lift very heavy prey into the air. (Some eagles can even fly away with prey that weighs more than they do.)

Sometimes, an eagle is able to take advantage of natural currents of air to help it rise. When wind runs into a hill or a mountain, it is forced upward—and the eagle can go along for the ride. This kind of air current is called *a slope updraft.*

When an eagle first leaves the ground, it gains altitude by flapping its wings. The flapping motion causes air to flow faster over the top of the wings, and the bird rises.

Coverts make the wing thicker in front, so that air will flow faster over the top of the wing.

Primary Feathers can be spread out like the fingers on a hand to reduce drag.

Secondary Feathers can be moved down to increase drag, or up to reduce it.

Scientists divide the feathers of an eagle's wing into groups. Each group has a different role to play in helping an eagle to fly, as shown above.

Most eagles have wings that are rather long and wide, to help them soar and glide with less effort. At low speeds, broad wings can hold a bird up in the air longer than narrow wings. And broad wings provide extra lift when an eagle has to carry its prey up into the air.

Swift   Eagle

Soaring high above the earth on motionless wings, an eagle is in the perfect place to see prey below on the ground. All eagles have wonderful eyes that can focus on small objects at long distances. An eagle can probably see a rabbit two miles away.

To rise really high into the air, eagles often hitch a ride on rising bubbles of hot air called "thermals." Once an eagle gets into a thermal, it can just spread its wings and float upward with very little effort, as explained below:

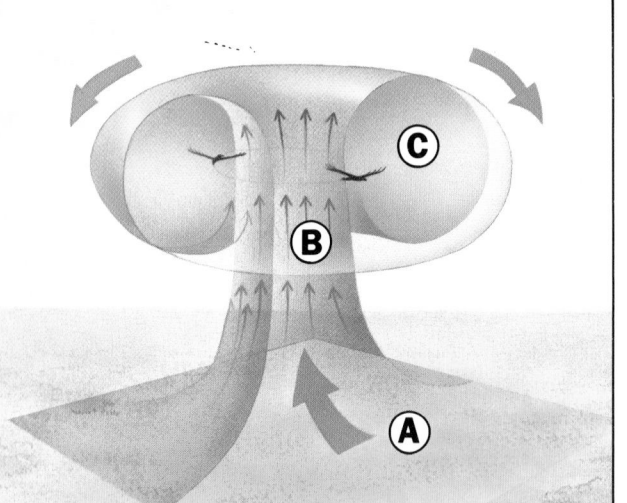

Thermals are formed when the sun warms the air near the ground (A). Hot air is lighter than cold air, as you know from watching steam rise out of a tea kettle. So the heated air rises (B). Eagles place themselves in the middle of the rising air and float upward with it (C). When a thermal is big, the eagles may climb to 3 miles above the earth (5 kilometers).

The ability of eyes to focus on objects at a distance is called "resolving power." Eagle eyes have resolving power that can be *8 times better* than the resolving power of human eyes.

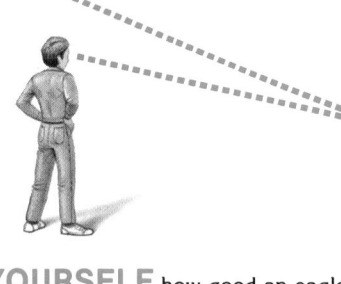

SEE FOR YOURSELF how good an eagle's eyes can be. Get a spool, or something else that is about one inch long (3 centimeters). Put the spool down on the ground and start backing away from it. When you can't see the spool anymore, you have reached the limits of your eyes' resolving power. Measure the distance and multiply by 8—and you will know how far away an eagle could be and still see the spool.

SEE FOR YOURSELF how the wide wings of many eagles make it easier for them to stay up in the air. Get two pieces of paper the same size. Fold one as shown below. Drop both pieces at the same time from the same height. See how the narrow paper drops faster than the wide paper, even though they both weigh the same.

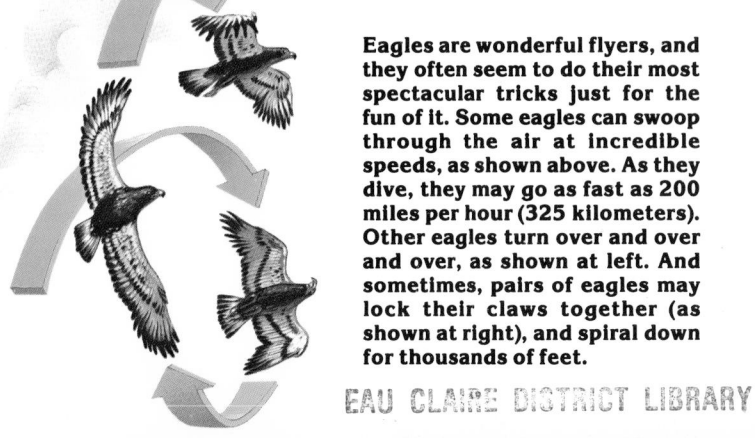

Eagles are wonderful flyers, and they often seem to do their most spectacular tricks just for the fun of it. Some eagles can swoop through the air at incredible speeds, as shown above. As they dive, they may go as fast as 200 miles per hour (325 kilometers). Other eagles turn over and over and over, as shown at left. And sometimes, pairs of eagles may lock their claws together (as shown at right), and spiral down for thousands of feet.

13

The Philippine Monkey-Eating Eagle is the second largest eagle in the world. Most eagles have yellow, orange or brown eyes, but this eagle has blue eyes.

Getting food is usually easy for eagles. They are so good at it that they often spend only a few hours a day hunting. After that, they may spend the rest of the day loafing. Or they may soar into the air and do tricks to amuse themselves.

Often, the bodies and hunting methods of eagles are specialized in some way for the kind of prey they hunt. As shown below, the claws and feet of many eagles are just the right size and shape for taking their prey.

Eagles don't always swoop down on their prey at great speed. Instead, they may simply spread their wings wide and float slowly down—dropping out of the sky so silently that the prey can't hear them coming.

Snake eagles have short, strong toes—just the thing for holding on to wriggling snakes. The snakes are usually swallowed whole.

Some booted eagles catch small prey. They have smaller toes and claws. Tawny eagles often go after Rock hyrax.

Other booted eagles take larger prey, so they have larger feet and claws. Crowned eagles often hunt monkeys.

Bald eagles are fish eagles. They usually catch fish by flying low over the water and snatching the fish out of the water with their talons. This method is only good for taking fish that are swimming close to the surface.

Fish eagles and Sea eagles have rough bumps on their toes to help them hold on to slippery fish.

Harpy eagles have huge claws that can be used for grabbing very big prey. The talons may be 5 inches long (13 centimeters). Harpies sometimes hunt deer.

During the coldest part of winter, eagles that live in the far north sometimes have trouble finding prey. At such times, they will eat just about any kind of meat they can find. In Alaska, Bald eagles may even show up at a dump to look for bits of human food.

Some eagles let other birds do their hunting for them. They wait until pelicans, herons, or other birds make a catch—and then steal the catch from them. Here, an African Fish eagle is about to pounce on a pelican. In order to escape, the pelican will drop the food from its mouth.

As a rule, eagles hunt alone or in pairs. But when there is a lot of food in one place, many eagles may gather to feed together. Bald eagles in Alaska gather by the hundreds when salmon are running in the rivers. The salmon are weak from their long swim upstream and are easy to capture.

Large eagles can hit their prey very hard. A Bald eagle can strike with *twice* the force of a rifle bullet.

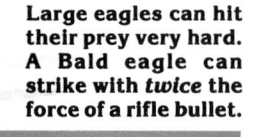

As powerful as they are, eagles aren't as big as most people think they are. An average Bald eagle weighs about 9 pounds (4 kilograms)—or *2 pounds less* than an average house cat.

Different kinds of foods are eaten by different kinds of eagles. As a rule, eagles prefer to eat live prey — animals that they have caught for themselves. Some types of eagles will eat almost any kind of live prey they can find. Others usually eat only a few kinds of live prey. Snake eagles, for instance, will stick to snakes when they can get them, with a few frogs and lizards once in a while.

When live prey is hard to find, some species of eagles will eat other things. The most common thing for them to eat at such times is carrion (CARRY-un) — animals that were already dead when the eagle found them.

Most eagles like to hunt from a perch. This is especially true of fish eagles and eagles that live in forests. Instead of flying around looking for prey, they sit on a branch or a stump and wait for prey to come along. Then they swoop down on it. Mated pairs of eagles often share their food, as the Philippine eagles below are doing. One of them has caught a wild jungle fowl.

To catch a big fish, eagles will sometimes plunge right into the water with a big splash. The African Fish eagle below is using its wings to keep a fish from escaping.

Tawny eagles of Africa probably eat more different kinds of food than any other eagle species. They feed on everything from locusts and termites to dead elephants. As shown above, they sometimes break open large ostrich eggs.

Bonelli's eagles are able to capture prey while flying *upside down*. They swoop in under a flying bird, roll over, and grab the bird in their talons. But this is very unusual. Most eagles like to drop on their prey from above. And most of them prefer to catch prey that is on the ground or in the water.

Once an eagle has captured its prey, it usually flies up into a tree with it. The eagle is safer eating on a branch than it would be on the ground. For this reason, most eagles take prey that is smaller and lighter than they are—prey that can be easily lifted into the air.

When eagles catch live prey, they keep all the food for themselves, their mates, and their young. But when they feed on carrion, they often have to share the food with other animals. The African Fish eagle below is sharing the meat of a dead hippo with a hyena.

In east Africa, Tawny eagles even hunt flamingoes. The eagles usually attack when the big pink birds are flying in a flock.

Of all the eagles, Palm-nut eagles have the strangest eating habits. They do not usually capture prey. Instead, they use their sharp beaks to crack open the nuts on palm trees, and eat the oily food inside.

Baby eagles are small and helpless when they are hatched. But they don't stay that way for long. All eagle parents take very good care of their young, and this includes feeding the eaglets all the food they can eat. As a result, the chicks grow very rapidly. Golden eagles, for example, weigh only about three ounces at birth (85 grams). But they weigh *forty times as much* only 45 days later.

On these pages, we've shown how Golden eagles bring their young into the world. Other types of eagles build different kinds of nests, and there may be some differences in the way they raise their young. But the story is basically the same for all baby eagles.

After mother eagles lay their eggs, they may sit on the nest for a long time before the eggs begin to hatch. The Golden eagle shown here may have to stay on the nest as long as 50 days. The job is sometimes shared by the father eagle.

Ⓐ

When a Golden eagle chick is ready to start hatching, it can be heard calling from inside the egg.

Ⓑ

After it starts calling, it takes the chick about 15 hours to peck the first hole in the egg. There is a special "egg tooth" on the chick's beak to break through the shell.

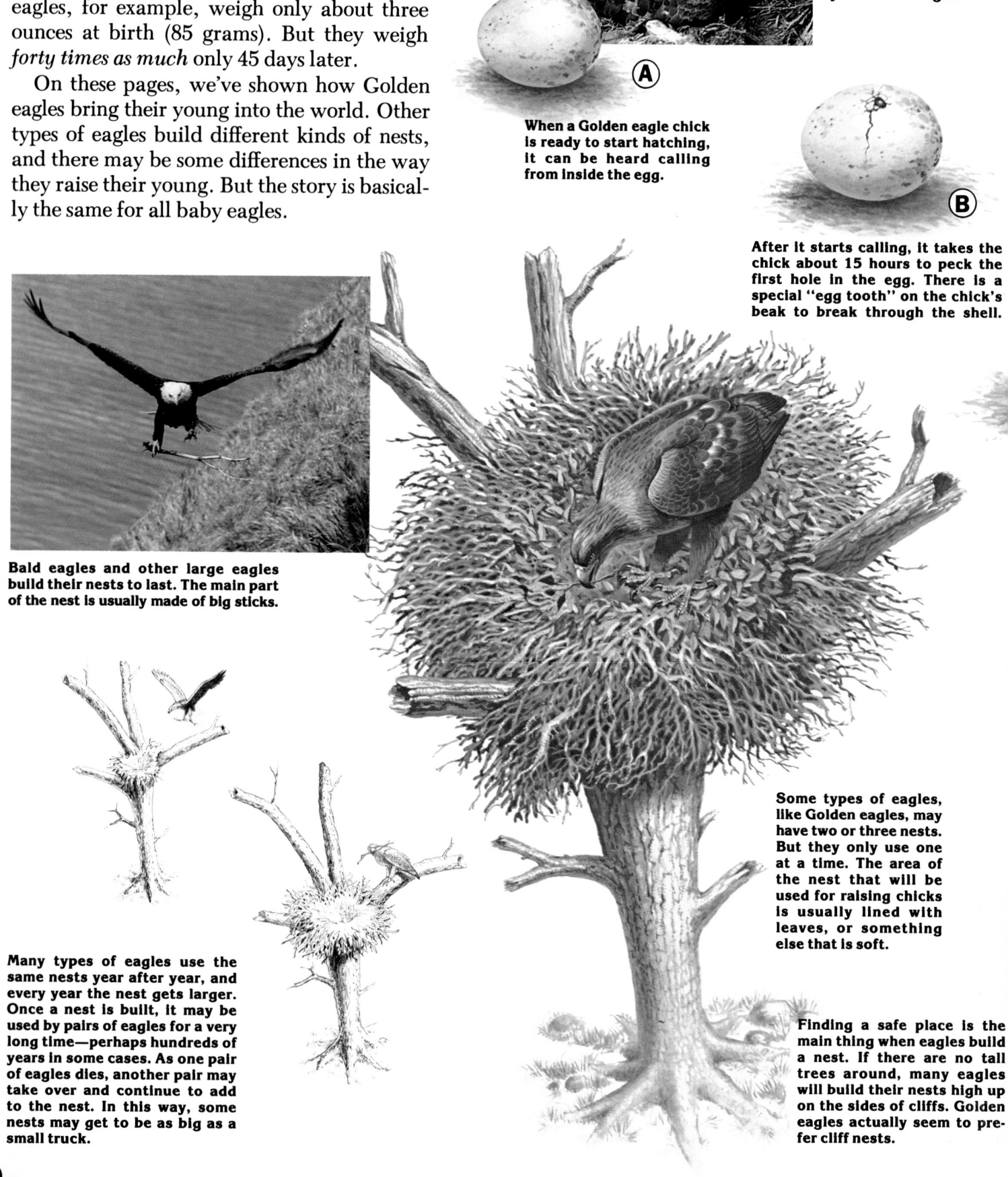

Bald eagles and other large eagles build their nests to last. The main part of the nest is usually made of big sticks.

Many types of eagles use the same nests year after year, and every year the nest gets larger. Once a nest is built, it may be used by pairs of eagles for a very long time—perhaps hundreds of years in some cases. As one pair of eagles dies, another pair may take over and continue to add to the nest. In this way, some nests may get to be as big as a small truck.

Some types of eagles, like Golden eagles, may have two or three nests. But they only use one at a time. The area of the nest that will be used for raising chicks is usually lined with leaves, or something else that is soft.

Finding a safe place is the main thing when eagles build a nest. If there are no tall trees around, many eagles will build their nests high up on the sides of cliffs. Golden eagles actually seem to prefer cliff nests.

When there are young eagles in the nest, both of the parents have to do a lot of hunting. The chicks never seem to get enough to eat, and their parents are constantly taking off to look for food.

From the time they hatch, it takes Golden eagles 65 to 75 days to get ready to fly. During this time, their white downy coats are replaced by darker feathers.

C

Once the first hole has been made, the chick starts working harder. But it may still take another 35 to 40 hours for it to break out of the shell completely.

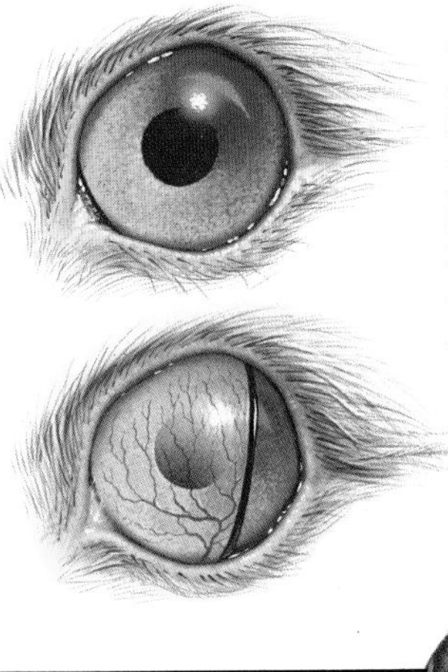

The eyes of all eagles have an extra eyelid called a nictitating membrane (NICK-tuh-TATE-ing). This can be used to clean the eyes or to protect them. Eagle parents often pull the membranes over their eyes when feeding their young. This keeps the chicks from accidentally damaging an eye as they lunge for food.

D

By the time the chick is all the way out of the shell, it is usually very tired. Most chicks lie still and rest for a bit, while they dry off and their feathers begin to fluff up.

Baby eagles don't drink milk like baby humans. Instead, their parents give them little bits of meat. The parents feed newborn chicks by gently placing the bits of meat in their mouths.

21

The future of eagles and the future of people are tied together. If we humans can learn to take better care of the earth, and to preserve at least some of its wild places, there will always be eagles. But if we do not, then many types of eagles will surely die out.

Strange as it may seem, these powerful creatures can be very easily hurt by things that people do. Even stranger is the fact that the things we admire most about eagles are often the same things that make them so vulnerable, so easy to hurt.

For example, we admire the size of some eagles—but size can be a problem for eagles. Big birds need big areas in which to hunt. And so, when people destroy forests or take land to build things on it, the eagles are the first to suffer. Other animals may be able to get along with smaller territories, but eagles can't.

We also admire the way that eagles can fly and hunt—but this can mean trouble for eagles, too. Many times, the prey that eagles eat can help to poison them. This happens when farmers use poisons to kill insects on their crops, or when factories pollute air and water. Small animals and fish take in the poisons. And when eagles eat the animals and fish, they also eat the poison. As the eagles continue to hunt, they take in more and more poison.

The skill of eagles as hunters has also made trouble for them with sheep ranchers and chicken farmers. In the past, many sheep ranchers in

the western United States were convinced that Golden eagles and Bald eagles were killing large numbers of lambs. As a result, rewards were paid for dead eagles and thousands were shot.

After a time, scientists were called in to study the problem. They found that eagles eat very few lambs and few chickens. Golden eagles prefer to eat rabbits and other small mammals. And Bald eagles eat fish most of the time. The fact is, eagles simply aren't big enough to carry away a lamb that is more than a month old.

One of the interesting things that scientists have discovered is that eagles don't really eat very much of anything. Many people think that eagles will eat everything they can catch, but this isn't true. An eagle usually eats only about *5 to 10 percent* of its own body weight in food each day. This means that a Bald eagle weighing 9 pounds eats *less than a pound of food a day* — hardly enough to cause serious damage to any group of animals.

It is sad to say that even the *beauty* of eagles can be dangerous for them. Sometimes, people who want to see eagles disturb them when they are nesting. This may cause the eagles to flee from the nest, leaving their eggs to grow cold.

The scientific study of eagles is showing us what eagles need to survive. We must make sure that poisons don't hurt them. We must keep thoughtless people from disturbing them. And most of all, we must leave enough wild places for them to live in.

Index